THE CHEERFUL WARRIOR

The Life of Charles Garnier

Written by

CHARLES DOLLEN

Illustrated by
the Daughters of St. Paul
under the direction of
Guy R. Pennisi

ST. PAUL EDITIONS

NIHIL OBSTAT:

JOHN R. QUINN, S.T.L.

IMPRIMATUR:

+ FRANCIS J. FUREY
Bishop of San Diego

Library of Congress Catalog Card Number 67-31067

Copyright, 1967, by the *Daughters of St. Paul*

for

Charles Joseph Gasse
and his twin
Paul Andre Gasse

CONTENTS

CHAPTER 1

A CENTURY OF HEROES

The saints are not sad. They are men and women who have caught sight of their homeland, and they know that the delights of Heaven are well within reach. We know that St. Philip Neri was the joy of Rome because of his light-heartedness, and every picture of St. Louise de Marillac shows her with a merry twinkle in her eye.

Of all the happy warriors in the Kingdom of God, it would be difficult to find one with a better sense of humor than the Parisian-born Charles Garnier. His spontaneous wit and his genuine laugh made him a hero among his schoolmates, a leader in the Jesuit novitiate, and a much sought out companion among the missionaries in the Huron territory of Canada.

He was born in Paris at the beginning of the seventeenth century. France at that time was the most powerful nation in the world. Its court life was brilliant and colorful, but unfortunately, the country was wracked with religious turmoil.

13

This was the century when France gave to the Church and the world so many saints and saintly people. During the lifetime of Charles Garnier, he would meet or hear about St. Francis de Sales, St. Jane Frances Fremiot de Chantal, St. Vincent de Paul, St. Louise de Marillac, Father Olier, Cardinal de Berulle and Bishop Bossuet.

This was also the century of Richelieu, Mazarin, Louis XIV, "The Sun King," and civil war in France. Outside of France, this was the time of the beheading of Charles I of England, and the dictatorship of Oliver Cromwell. Father Matteo Rici, the Jesuit, was at work in Peking making great progress among the Mandarins. In Rome, the Galileo controversy exploded and St. Robert Bellarmine had to come to the scientist's rescue.

"But the most exciting things that are happening," Charles told his classmates, "are happening in the New World."

"Just think of all those savage Indians."

"And all the golden cities that the Spanish are finding."

No wonder that the young people of Paris could look forward to adventure and challenge in their lives.

"It's a huge new land across the ocean," they were told. "It must not be left to Spain and Portugal alone."

"Where can France find a share?" was the question that began to bother everyone at the French court.

Sixty years before this, Spain and Portugal had claimed the entire New World, and they had divided it up between themselves. At that time, no one realized that there were two whole continents in the Americas. Europe was going through the terrible religious wars of the sixteenth century and most of the nations were more interested in conquering each other than in conquering a new world.

However, by the middle of the seventeenth century, England, Sweden, Holland and finally the French realized they had made a mistake. Only the northern areas of North America had not been settled by the Spanish and Portuguese colonizers. France claimed vast regions in what is now Canada and northeastern United States.

Then the French court found out that it could not encourage many people to go to New France. There were no gold mines such as were found in Mexico and Peru, the Indians were more warlike, and the climate was rugged.

"How can we hope to hold the land if we cannot find settlers?" the king asked.

"There are other riches there than gold," he was told. "Great fortunes can be made in the fur trade."

Soon, fur traders roamed far and wide over the top half of the continent. Their exports made Paris

the fur capital of Europe and it brought great fortunes to many French families. Missionaries were
soon invited to accompany the wandering traders.
Brave young French boys were dreaming of going
to New France in one capacity or the other

The Garnier family was engaged in the admin-
istrative work of the French government. They be-
longed to the upper middle class, just a step below
the nobility. Their class kept the court and the government going on a day to day basis.

Charles' father was the Secretary of the Grand
Council under King Henry III, and later he was
appointed the Treasurer of Normandy. Charles'
grandfather had been commander of the military
garrison at Pithiviers. During the civil war, the huge
forces of DeConde swept through the town and
captured the garrison. When Commander Garnier
refused to renounce his Catholic faith and join the
rebellion, he was put to death.

"Grandfather was a martyr for Christ," Charles
was told by his mother. "In my mind I'm certain
of it."

"He was a hero," replied Charles, and in his
heart, he determined to be equally heroic some day.

The Garnier family was deeply religious, completely devoted to Christ and His Church. Two of
the older boys became priests, one a Carmelite and
one a Capuchin. After Charles' death, the Carmelite
brother wrote a book about his brother's youth.

"Grandfather was a hero," replied
Charles, and in his heart, he determined
to be equally heroic some day.

His mischievousness, his pranks and practical jokes, as well as his youthful escapades with his buddies are all recorded. They would help themselves to fruit when they ran past a fruitstand. Once they "lifted" a chicken from a restaurant and had their own private banquet. When the senior Garnier heard about this, he delivered enough corporal punishment to Charles to keep this sort of amusement out of his life forever.

Charles grew up with all the excitement of youth in a big city. There were parades to watch, games to play, sports, school and outings. When there were big parties at the palace, Charles and his buddies would gather at the gate to watch the carriages move in. The royal balls were always colorful, and the men wore just as fancy clothes as the women.

"But there must be more to life than this," Charles told himself. He was a serious teenager for all his cheerfulness, and he wanted his life to have real meaning.

CHAPTER 2

THE YOUNG JESUIT

"What will I make of myself?" he mused.

"Do I want to make a great fortune and attend royal balls, all dressed up in silk?" He knew he didn't want that. Since he liked to read, he began studying the lives of the saints.

Unfortunately for Charles, biographies of the saints in those days always emphasized the unusual in their lives. Great penances and great miracles do not make great saints. God can use anyone He wants to do His work, even sinners. Saints are great because of their faith, hope and charity and because of the service they give to God and neighbor.

Charles had to find this out the hard way. He began multiplying his prayers until he was spending hours in private devotions, secretly, in his room. After school he would run off to the parish church for more prayers, until his schoolmates became suspicious.

"Where is Garnier now?" one would ask.

"I don't know. He took off that way."

"Tomorrow we will follow him," they decided.

The next day they followed Charles to the church. They played around outside until he came out.

"Do we have a new desert Father here?" they asked.

"I'm just praying for you," Charles told them, laughing. "I couldn't think of anyone who needed it more!"

Finally he talked with a kindly Jesuit priest.

"My friends laugh at me, but when I read about my patron, St. Charles Borromeo, I find that he was always praying."

"Of course," said the priest. "Our Lord told us that we should 'pray always,' but He meant that our whole life must be a prayer. Everything we do, we do for Christ and in Christ."

"Your fun, your sports, your school—do all these as a Christian and you will be praying."

During this time Charles also discovered the works of charity. His father was very generous with an allowance, and Charles began to give most of it to the Indian missions. Already he was beginning to be attracted to his future apostolate.

One unusual "charity" that Charles tried is recorded by his brother. Since Charles loved to read, he spent many hours in the used-book stores for which Paris is still famous. When he noticed a bad book on the stalls, he would buy it and destroy it. "So that it will not do harm to souls," he would say.

"Do we have a new desert Father
here?" they asked.

His Jesuit friend corrected him gently. "That is the negative approach, Charles. It is important to be positive, too, by spreading good books, and encouraging their production."

The conditions in the French jails were deplorable and when this was brought to Charles' attention, he determined to do something about it. He organized visits to the prisoners, and he and his companions brought along food and simple first-aid remedies. It wasn't much, but it was the best they could do. A few years later, Louise de Marillac and her Ladies of Charity made this a part of their mission.

At this time, Charles was a member of the Sodality of Our Lady, a Jesuit-sponsored group for youth. The Sodality offers many spiritual benefits to young people, and it has the added advantage of obtaining for them some good, spiritual direction.

"The Sodality is only for serious people," one of his brothers said.

"Youth is more serious than adults give us credit for," he answered easily, and he continued to be an active Sodalist.

When ready for college, his father enrolled him at the Jesuit school of Louis le Grand. This college had been founded to train the sons of the nobility, but the Garnier family was so respected at court that Charles was welcomed by all.

"I'll make no secret of it, my son," his father told him. "With your two older brothers in religious orders, I want you to continue the fame and fortunes of the Garnier name."

"Many high positions in government will be open to you," said his mother, "and we want you to have every advantage."

"For the first time," the father added quietly, "there is a chance for a Garnier to enter the nobility."

This was certainly a legitimate ambition in the France of that time. The nobility always impressed on the upper middle class the great gap that existed between their positions. This could not have but hurt so loyal a civil servant as the senior Garnier.

Sometime later Charles received a letter from his father.

"Mademoiselle Genevieve would make you a fine wife. Besides being beautiful both in body and soul, she has wealth and excellent political connections."

When Charles read this, he sat down and wrote to his father immediately.

"Please try to understand, but I want to become a Jesuit missionary. Every day I feel more and more attracted to New France and the work among the Indians."

It came as no surprise to Charles that his parents finally accepted his decision. Being such fine Catholics, they realized what a privilege it was to have a third son called to the priesthood. The young lady also followed Charles' example and became a nun at the famous convent of Port Royale.

The Jesuits received Charles into their Parisian novitiate on September 5, 1624. He was not quite twenty years old. His first year as a novice passed quickly and happily, and soon he was ready to make the required pilgrimage.

"You will take nothing with you," the novice master reminded his young group, "and you will live on the alms for which you beg."

In small groups of two's and three's they set out. Each little group could chose a separate shrine, and Charles and his friends set out for Pithiviers to visit the place of his grandfather's death.

After professing his vows as a Jesuit, Charles was sent back to the College of Louis le Grand to study philosophy and theology. Here he met many of the Company with whom he would be working in New France. The missionaries who were returning from the new world would stop and bring reports from the field.

"Father Isaac Jogues is leaving for Lake Champlain and the regions south of Ontario."

"Father John Brebeuf is moving ever westward in his search for souls."

All of this fired up the minds and imagination of these young men. They were determined to offer themselves for this great work.

At the college, Garnier first met the future Father Chastelain, and they became the best of friends. They seem to have been attracted to each other right from the start. They were comrades in

Sometime later Charles received a letter from his father.

spirit and work for the rest of their lives. A friend is an other-self, and these two young men found themselves in each other.

In such enjoyable companionship, Charles spent the next few years preparing for his ordination. They were years of hard work and much study, but they were happy years. Chastelain excelled in theology, while Garnier was better at the secular subjects. Around exam time, they could always be seen studying together, trading questions and answers.

Finally the great day of ordination arrived, and surrounded by their families and relatives, they became priests of God, forever.

CHAPTER 3

FATHER GARNIER, S. J.

When the great French explorer, Champlain, returned to France, he had tales of discovery and fortune to tell at the court. The news swept across France and everyone was excited about it.

"Thousands of square miles—ours for the taking!" he said.

"We must beat the English to it."

"Unlimited fur trade!"

Richelieu tried to put a stop to the talk. "We do not want savage land," he declared. "The destiny of France is to lead Europe."

Richelieu had joined with Sweden to defeat the Holy Roman Emperor and to check the power of Austria. Secretly he wanted to make war on Spain and put an end to the last great competitor to France's leadership in Europe. He was not interested in spending money on explorations or sending men to America.

"Richelieu," said the king, "the future will be decisively shaped by the new world. We command you to take lands there in the name of France."

Reluctantly, the prime minister agreed, but his heart was never in it. He wanted immediate grandeur for France. The king was looking to the future, but he, unfortunately, was more interested in the parties and balls and he did not follow up on his command.

The French people, however, were enthusiastic about it. They listened to the stories of the Indians of the north, people engulfed in strange and even degrading religious practices. Champlain described the pagan war dances, the tortures and the ruthlessness of these vast Indian nations.

The fact that there were countless souls waiting to hear the good news of salvation in Christ was enough for the French Jesuits. They all volunteered to go.

"Good," said the Jesuit superior. "We will send as many men as we can spare."

On April 5, 1636, four Jesuits left Dieppe for the trip to New France. They were Father Isaac Jogues, superior, and Fathers Chastelain, Daniel and Garnier. The new governor, Montmagny, was also on board.

The ship was commanded by General Bouchard. Today we would give him the rank of Admiral, but France was always army-minded, so he was called a "General of the Fleet."

"I am delighted to have four priests on board," he told the Jesuits.

"It will be a rough voyage, but I will do everything I can to make it pleasant for you."

He was a devout Catholic, and whenever the ocean was calm enough to permit the celebration of Mass, he attended. Quite frequently he served Mass. He turned his own quarters into a chapel and a catechetical center.

"It will be many, many weeks before we reach our destination," the General said, "so we will use our spare time to advantage."

He decreed that the sailors and the children of the colonists who were aboard were to receive daily religious instructions. The Jesuits were delighted to cooperate.

"Each of us will take a different class," Father Jogues said, "so that we can give more specialized instructions."

Father Garnier was given the older sailors to teach, and at first he met with quite a bit of silent opposition. One sailor in particular, described by Jogues as "tough and hairy," was determined to embarrass Garnier.

He delighted in tormenting the priest by his bad language, dirty jokes, and his state of undress. "I have nothing but contempt for religion!" he shouted one day.

"Priests are no good!" he screamed another time. "They lead soft lives and are paid from the sweat of the poor."

"I am sharing the same hardships as you on this voyage," Charles answered calmly, "and in New France I will be living on the frontier."

"Priests don't know what hard work is!"

"When you are safely back in Paris," the priest responded, "I will be crouching over a fire in a primitive hut."

Before the voyage was half over, Charles' patience and good nature had won the man over. Father Garnier's easy laughter and his willingness to work on any challenge was too much for the old salty sailor. He became a good practicing Catholic for all the rest of his life.

On the feast of the apostle St. Barnabas, June 11, 1636, the ship anchored in the beautiful St. Lawrence River off the majestic Quebec Rock. It had been a speedy voyage lasting a little over two months. The same journey today, by jet aircraft, takes only a few hours.

The settlers at Quebec rushed down to meet the newcomers. There was a general celebration to honor the arrival of Champlain's successor.

"An adult Indian is to be baptized today," they told the new priests.

"Would one of the new priests like to do it?"

"I would," cried Father Chastelain.

"Who will be the sponsor?" asked Charles Garnier.

The new governor settled it. "I would like to be the Indian's godfather. The spread of the Christian

One sailor in particular was determined
to embarrass Garnier. "I have nothing but
contempt for religion!" he shouted one day.

faith is more important to me than the spread of the fur trade. I want all the colonists to understand that."

They were introduced to the young man. He was almost trembling with anticipation.

"I want to take the name Joseph," he told the governor. "That saint was one of the closest to Our Lord Jesus Christ when he walked on the earth."

After the baptismal celebration, the newly arrived Jesuits settled down for a few weeks of on-the-spot training.

CHAPTER 4

THE NEW MISSIONARIES

"You have been assigned to the Huron nation," said Isaac Jogues one morning in late June.

Garnier and Chastelain were overjoyed to hear the news. Their new mission stations would be close together so they would continue to see each other often.

"When do we leave?" they asked excitedly.

"On July 1," was the answer.

They journeyed westward until they came to Three Rivers. They were welcomed by Father Le-Jeune, the local superior and he and the other Jesuits insisted that they stay for a few days.

"We are anxious to hear all the news about the Company of Jesus back in France," they said.

Garnier and Chastelain stayed for a full week. While there, Charles baptized his first Indian, a little baby. He felt like a real missionary, now, but his work had only begun.

They had been there five days when Father Daniel arrived. He had a large group of Indian boys with him.

"Whatever are you doing?" they asked in surprise.

"I am taking these young men back to Quebec to start a new Jesuit school," Daniel answered. "The decision was made after you left Quebec. When the messenger reached me, I was already prepared to come."

"These young priests are going to the new villages up the Ottawa River," Father LeJeune told Daniel.

This was the first that the two priests had heard of their actual assignment.

"These villagers have asked for Black Robes."

"How different from when we first arrived!" exclaimed some of the veterans.

When the Indians arrived with the canoes to transport the two priests, Father LeJeune insisted that they be given some practice in riding the Indian boats. The Indians courteously assisted the white men into the canoes. They wouldn't let them take off their shoes, which was a tremendous mark of respect.

"I've never seen them do that to a white man before," marvelled LeJeune.

"It's those two," said Daniel. "They're so cheerful and brimming with life that even the Indians are affected by it."

They would have been even more amazed if they could have seen the passage at the portages. When the Indians came to the rapids, it was cus-

While at Three Rivers, Charles baptized his first Indian,
a little baby. He felt like a real missionary now.

tomary for everyone in the boat to get out and help transport the baggage over the rapids until there was clear water again.

The Indians would not let the two Black Robes carry a thing. As they had journeyed up the river, the Indians had grown more and more fond of these two white men who seemed to have a kind word, a joke, or a smile for everyone.

"These men must know no fear," the Indians whispered in great wonderment.

"The God of the Christians must be very close to them," they said to one another.

The long journey continued. Finally they arrived at the outskirts of Huronia, the Isle des Allumettes. They were about one hundred miles north of the modern city of Toronto. They bought corn here, and pushed on, toward the northwest. It was on the feast of St. Ignatius, the founder of their order, that they arrived among the Huron Indians. The journey had taken them thirty-one days by canoe and on foot.

Ihonitiria was the local headquarters for the Jesuit mission in Huronia. Here they met the famous St. John Brebeuf, the local superior. He was as famous for his huge size as he was for his reputation for sanctity.

"Your first job," he told them, "is to learn the dialect of the tribes to which you will go."

They settled down to the task, eagerly, but it was a difficult one. On their third day, everyone was stricken with a mysterious illness, Jesuits and Indians alike.

"We thought we were all going to die," Charles wrote, "but we all recovered just as quickly and as mysteriously as we had been struck down."

Brebeuf wrote to Jogues, "This Garnier is a treasure. Without his help and his cheeriness, our morale would have gone completely. Send me more like him!"

Then he said to his fellow Black Robes, "I think this place is unhealthy. Let us scout around and find higher ground for our headquarters."

They chose the nearby village of Ossossane where the chief gave them a large plot of ground on the edge of town.

"We will build a permanent compound here," Brebeuf decided. "It must have a good sized chapel, a place to give instructions, living quarters and some enclosed land for a bit of privacy."

The Frenchmen set to work and the Indians helped them. The results were very primitive by European standards but the Hurons were very impressed with the buildings.

"It is a fortress," they said.

"This must be how they conquered their homeland."

"I'm glad they are our friends."

Charles was very amused by this simple misinterpretation, but when he wrote home, he had other amusing items to relate.

"They think I am very handsome," he told his father, "because I cannot raise a beard like the others. They feel very sorry for the Black Robes who have to scrape all that extra hair off their faces!"

The medical problems of the Indians really bothered the Jesuits.

"They are a sickly race," Brebeuf wrote back to Paris. "Every disease decimates their ranks, and their natural life span is very short. Can you send us some doctors?"

The shortage of doctors bothered all the missionaries. When they could recruit physicians these men usually preferred to live in the larger settlements of colonists. The only resort of the Black Robes was to teach their men simple medical remedies and good first-aid techniques.

Charles Garnier took to this almost instinctively. He had great skill at first aid, and, as he put it, "whether by the grace of God or simple good luck, I seem to be able to cure most of those brought to me."

The Indians, of course, considered him a superior medicine man who did not demand payment for his services. He did insist that they clean up their cabins but since they didn't understand why this was necessary, they never made more than half-hearted efforts at it. They knew what he would say when he came to minister to the sick, so they nicknamed him "Doctor Clean."

"I think they're afraid of your medical magic," joked Father Chastelain.

The Frenchmen set to work building the mission compound, and the Indians helped them.

"They think a simple clean bandage is a good health charm, but they don't try to keep clean," sighed Charles.

"They've got to learn," said Brebeuf. "They have great potential."

There was great natural potential in these native Americans of northern North America, as proved by how quickly and how well they responded to French teaching. The Spaniards also found that the Indians learned easily. By this time, there were several universities in Spanish America, colleges, monasteries and printing presses. The Spanish, particularly, absorbed the Indians into their culture, and were, in turn, absorbed by the Indians until a whole new culture resulted. The Mexicans, for instance, blended the best of both of their ancestors into a new nation.

CHAPTER 5

A WILLING WORK

"Why are we here?" John Brebeuf asked.

It was their first retreat Sunday after the two young Jesuits arrived. All the Black Robes in Huronia were gathered together for this spiritual exercise.

"We must see Christ in these Huron Indians. We serve Christ by serving these, the least of His brethren."

He looked around him. These Jesuits were men who had come from important families in France. Some came from the nobility; all were from families of wealth.

At home they could have looked forward to positions of influence and status. They could have married well and had political positions offered to them. They could have become priests at home and been given big parishes, become court chaplains or canons in some great cathedral.

Instead, they had made a dangerous journey across the ocean. Then they had left the small comforts of frontier settlements and trudged into the interior. They had no more comforts than their savage converts. Charles thought of the sailor who thought priests led easy lives.

"No sacrifice is too great," Brebeuf declared, "to reach these souls and bring them the grace of Baptism."

Again Brebeuf looked at them. These men had the finest education that Europe could offer. They had been shaped in the great Jesuit tradition. Yet, with all their learning, they were teaching the simplest of catechism lessons. They had to take a primitive language and teach deep spiritual lessons.

"The charity of Christ urges us on," was a text from St. Paul that inspired these missionaries. And, they knew a truth that Abbot Marmion was to write down two hundred and fifty years later. "You do not know your theology until you can teach a First Holy Communion class." Anyone can proclaim a mystery; only a man of God can translate it into active love.

About the only material consolation that these men had were the rather rare letters to and from home. Charles Garnier had a deep, abiding love for his homeland and his family. He was a Christian first, then a Jesuit, third a Frenchman, and definitely a Garnier.

He and his Carmelite brother kept up an extensive correspondence. Every time a messenger arrived from Quebec there was a letter for Charles, and whenever a messenger left Huronia, Charles had a letter ready to go. In a way, the Jesuit acted as a type of spiritual director for the Carmelite monk.

Charles' letters were filled with common sense, good humor and a deep spirituality. His outlook was positive and progressive. He showed a keen awareness of events going on in France. It is interesting to note that he was very fond of the writings of St. Francis de Sales.

"Read his books," Charles wrote his brother. "The great Bishop of Geneva knows how to combine moderation with progress."

The Jesuits had to use a simple, direct catechical method with the Hurons. They found that pictures were of great help in getting their message across. Charles frequently had his brother design special pictures for him.

"The pictures must be brilliant in color," he said, "and very graphic, very detailed."

For instance, when he wanted a series done about Christ, he described what he wanted.

"Christ must be simple, very manly, and partially undraped so the Indians can admire him. He must not have a beard, since the Indians consider it a flaw."

In another letter he talks about pictures of Our Lady.

"She must wear a bright crown. Her Son should be standing upright on her knee. Forget the halo.

The Indians think it is some kind of European hat.
However, you can have rays coming out from around
them. The Hurons often see the Northern Lights,
and they connect rays of light with the power of
divinity."

About this time, a new tribe of Indians arrived
in Huronia. They could have been from the area
near Niagara Falls.

"Who are they?" asked Chastelain.

"They are called the Neutrals," replied Garnier.
"The Hurons despise them because they did not fight
for their homelands."

"Who took the land away from them?"

"The Iroquois, of course."

They all shuddered. The Iroquois Nation of upstate New York had a fierce reputation. They were
determined to form a great Indian Empire, and they
had begun to move in on all their neighbors.

Already they despised the French. When the
Indians of present-day Quebec befriended Champlain, he had used his guns to help them repel an
Iroquois attack. They never forgot that. They dis-
trusted all white men, but their special hate was for
the French. This was the confederation of great
tribes to whom St. Isaac Jogues went to preach the
Gospel of salvation.

As often happens with neutrals, the Neutrals
were despised by both sides. The pagan Hurons

The Jesuits found that pictures were of great
help in teaching the Indians about Christ.

looked on with indifference as these poor displaced people tried to eke out a living in a strange land.

"We cannot let them die," said Brebeuf. "These are human beings who need help, and souls that need grace."

The Jesuits moved in among them with food and simple first aid. Charles, who discovered that he had a facility for learning Indian dialects, was soon able to converse with them.

"These poor wretches," he exclaimed to his brethren. "What tortures they have undergone. Some of them were tortured for days and just kept alive long enough for the next day's torture. They were finally left for dead."

Some had limbs missing. Many had been mutilated. All were starving and in a state of stupor. Then the bad news came.

"The plague, the plague!"

"Some of them have the plague!"

Then even the Jesuits were afraid. Back in the Europe of the seventeenth century the plague still sometimes wiped out whole villages. When it entered a big city, thousands would die overnight.

Medical science of the time was helpless in the face of the plague, and all these missionaries had was first aid. They knew they were beaten.

The superstitious Indians blamed the Black Robes.

"We told you," said the medicine men. "They pretended to help us, but their medicine is really witchcraft."

"Their prayers are evil incantations," said the sorcerers.

The local chiefs were powerless to restrain the medicine men and the sorcerers. They went among the people, stirring them up with their chants.

"The old gods are seeking their revenge."

"See, the Christians cannot stop the power of our gods who are punishing us."

John Brebeuf gathered the missionaries around him. It was late October, 1637. They met in the chapel at Ossossane.

"We must face the fact of martyrdom," he told them solemnly. "At any moment they may march against us."

The silent forest around them seemed to bristle with hostility.

"We are not men of blood, so we will not fire against them," said Brebeuf. "Anyone who wants to leave has permission to sneak out."

"No," said Chastelain. "We are ready to die for Christ!"

They all chorused agreement. "If necessary, we will die for Christ."

Brebeuf was silent for a moment. Then he decided. "All right. Let us write a letter to Quebec to explain our stand."

They composed the letter together, and they told their superiors that they accepted the expected death in the spirit of heroic charity, offering their lives for their flock.

The letter was signed by Fathers John Brebeuf, Francis Le Mercier, Pierre Chastelain, Charles Garnier, Paul Ragueneau and, in a postscript, the names Pierre Pijart and Isaac Jogues were added.

CHAPTER 6

EXPANSION

Each night during that seemingly endless month of October, the Jesuits went to bed not knowing whether or not there was a mob ready to jump them under cover of darkness. This time, however, the mood passed, and the Indians settled down for the long winter.

Then one day the cry went up, "Iroquois, Iroquois!"

A war party was scouting the neighborhood for the war that seemed inevitable between the Hurons and the Iroquois.

"They have attacked our fishing party!"

"All our young men are killed!"

The villagers raced down to the river. About a dozen young Hurons had been fishing when the Iroquois surprised them. The two sons of the village medicine man were involved in the fight.

The older son, a young brave approaching the vigor of manhood, fought with savage skill to save

49

his younger brother. They were trying to capture the youngster alive to keep him as a slave.

"My brother fought like a wild bear," the younger boy recounted. "When they finally cut him down, he fell over me and told me to play dead."

By the time help arrived from the village, the older brother was gasping for breath, vainly trying to hold on to life. He had been under instruction, and when Charles took him in his arms, the young man begged for baptism.

"Get me water," the priest commanded. Someone raced to get him a gourd full of water.

"I baptize you in the name of the Father, and of the Son and of the Holy Spirit," prayed Garnier, as he poured the water over the young man's brow. No sooner was he baptized than he died in St. Charles' arms.

A few weeks later, the daughter of this same medicine man contacted a pestilence and lay dying.

"Send for the Black Robe," she begged.

Her father looked at her in anger. "He shall never enter here."

But the first time that both of her parents were absent, she sent her younger brother to bring the priest. As he approached her, Charles could see that she would not live out the day.

"Baptize me, baptize me," she whispered. "I want to be with my older brother in Heaven."

When Charles finished giving her the Sacrament, her parents returned. They shouted and

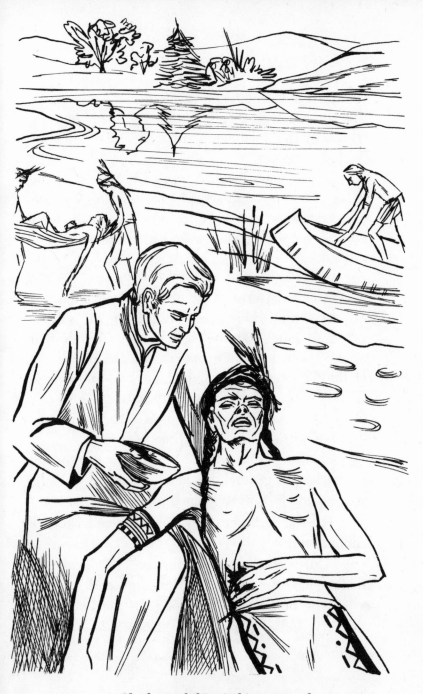

Charles took him in his arms and
the young man begged for Baptism.

screamed at Garnier, and finally threw him outside. The girl died peacefully within the hour, but the hatred of this medicine man followed Charles for the rest of his life.

On the other hand, it seemed as if most of the villagers had come to accept Charles. They enjoyed his personality and they seemed to take him for himself, forgetting that he was a white man and a foreigner.

When he talked about "The Prayer," as the pagans called Christianity, most listened attentively, even if they didn't accept his message. It is interesting to note that the side of the Church that most appealed to these Indians was the prayer life of the Christian. The same thing was true over a century later when Christianity entered the heart of Africa. We read in the life of St. Charles Lwanga that a Christian was called "one who prays."

Charles was on familiar terms with everyone in his village. In general, he could come and go as he pleased and he was welcomed in most families.

Then in October 1640, John Brebeuf called a conference.

"Our work prospers here," he said, "and now that we have more men, we should expand."

"The next nation west of us is the Petuns, or Tobacco Indians," Pierre Chastelain said in agreement.

"We must send two veteran missionaries," put in Isaac Jogues, who was now with the men in Huronia.

Before Brebeuf could ask for volunteers, all the priests were asking permission to go to the Petuns. He decided to send Isaac Jogues and Charles Garnier.

"I am sorry to send you among strangers who may be hostile and right at the beginning of winter, but it's the best we can do," he told them.

"If we go in spring or summer," replied Jogues, "the hunting season is on and all the tribes are on the move."

"We must start now," Charles agreed. "I hope we can get some Indian guides to go with us."

Not a single brave would go with the Frenchmen. They all predicted that the Petuns would kill the white men without even listening to them. However Isaac and Charles were determined to go, even if they had to go alone.

They started out for the beautiful land that is now, roughly, the western part of the province of Ontario, Canada. It stretches out from the shores of Lake Huron to the magnificence of Georgian Bay. It was a cold and hostile land to the first two Christians to enter it.

The Petuns met the missionaries with studied indifference. They simply ignored them. The priests were refused lodging, and no one would sell them corn.

"Well," said Charles, with a smile, "I suppose it's better than what we were told to expect."

"Yes," replied Jogues. "Everyone said we'd be killed."

The Black Robes travelled about from village to village. They named each one for an Apostle. Their hardships were great and many, and there were days when all they had to eat was the bark of trees. In the freezing cold and snow of a northern winter, they had to sleep outside, on the ground.

Still they went about their work. In each village, they looked for the sick, to give them medicine and, when desired, baptism. Since most of these sick people died soon after, the medicine men spread the word that the Black Robes practiced black magic.

By the middle of winter, the Jesuits were shut out of every village. If they came close to a Petun settlement, the children would set up a howl, and the braves would come toward them menacingly. When they fell ill in the face of such hostility, they were left to lie on the ground to die.

At this point, a Christian Indian named Joseph Chiwatenwa, came from St. Mary's Residence looking for them.

"Thank God!" cried Jogues. He was weeping.

"It's divine Providence that sent you," murmured Charles, wanly.

When no messages came through from the two missionaries, Brebeuf had become alarmed.

There were days when all they had
to eat was the bark of trees.

"Pierre," he said to Chastelain, "see if you can hear any rumors in the village about their journey."

Father Chastelain pieced together the rumors and found that the two priests had not been put to death, but that they were in the gravest of danger. Then Brebeuf sent Joseph to tell them to return to Ossossane. The mission to the tobacco-growing Petuns would be continued another time.

SEVEN YEARS OF GRACE

"A Christian like Joseph Chiwatenwa makes all of this work worthwhile," Pierre Chastelain said to Charles one day.

"Yes, indeed," he answered. "Every tribe in the Huron nation has some of these converts who are making real progress in the spiritual life."

Not only did these men and women accept Christianity, they became the finest witnesses to Christ and to Christian charity among their own people. Another outstanding example was Catherine or Kateri Tekawitha, a young Indian maiden who became an example of Christian love for all her tribe.

"What natural potential these people have," the Jesuits marvelled. "With the help of supernatural grace, what saints they can become!"

Convinced that the grace of God was active among the Indians, the Frenchmen were encouraged to continue their efforts.

"We must try to reach the Petuns again," Brebeuf declared.

"This time, let us go better prepared," replied Charles.

Garnier and Father Pierre Pijart returned to the villages of the Apostles, as they liked to call them. This time, messages had been sent ahead, and the missionaries took ample supplies with them. They still could not get any of the Hurons to accompany them.

Boldly advancing, the Jesuits demanded the privilege of addressing the assemblage of the chiefs. Amazed by the bravery of the Black Robes, the chiefs agreed to listen to them.

After their presentation, the chiefs discussed it among themselves. Finally they decided.

"You are free to come and go as you please. You may buy corn and you may sleep inside. No more than that."

Charles was overjoyed. "We're making progress."

However, he was overly optimistic. As they wandered about the villages they made a few friends in the village of St. John, but otherwise nothing. Brebeuf decided that they were more needed in Huronia, so once again he recalled them.

As they were leaving, a very strange experience occurred. Both Garnier and Pijart wrote about it several times.

"It was the middle of winter and the snow was up to our waists. A group of young braves, probably drugged, fell upon us and threw us to the ground."

Boldly advancing, the Jesuits demanded the
privilege of addressing the assemblage of the chiefs.

"Yet a second time," wrote Charles, "I expected death among the Petuns, and I offered myself for their conversion. But then, something happened. We were helpless under them. The death blow was in evidence. However, the whole band looked up, saw something, and ran off, scared and howling."

The two Jesuits attributed their escape to their Guardian Angels, a devotion which was strong among the Canadian Jesuits.

Back in Huronia, Charles was now considered both a hero and a veteran missionary. His joyful spirit seemed to pave the way for conversion.

"He tells a joke," said Chastelain, "and six more adults come to class."

"No," he replied, "it's just that we are learning to trust the Indians more. They make excellent Christians."

"How fearful we were," agreed Father Lalemant, "that they wouldn't persevere."

"Well, it made us more careful in giving them more thorough instruction," added Pierre Chastelain.

"You know," Gabriel Lalemant mused, "before we understood their customs, we thought many things they did were sinful."

"Right," said Charles. "Some of their actions seem crude to us, but we can not impose European customs on them."

During these seven years, Garnier worked in every mission station in Huronia. Brebeuf seemed

to depend on him to fill in wherever there was a
need. Among his brethren he was regarded with real
love, and his appearance was welcomed with en-
thusiasm.

He worked among the sick untiringly. His little
bag of medical supplies was always with him. He
was especially devoted to the children, and he
gathered them around him for catechism at every
opportunity. Like his patron, St. Charles Borromeo,
he considered religious education a most important
part of a priest's life.

During all this time, his own spiritual life was
growing. From his letters, it is apparent that his
prayer life was approaching the mystical.

"I am so aware," he wrote, "of the constant pre-
sence of God in me and around me."

And another time he wrote, "Daily I beg God
for the gift of martyrdom. I offer my blood to water
the ground for a new harvest of souls."

He remembered the ancient Christian saying,
"The blood of martyrs is the seed of Christians."

In 1648 he returned to the Petuns for another
attempt at converting that nation. This time, two
villages received him, the village of St. John and the
village of St. Matthias. However, these little settlements were so poor that they could not afford to
feed two visitors.

Father Brebeuf wrote to Garnier and his companion, Father Noel Chabanel. "Father Chabanel

must return to Huronia, but Father Garnier may remain if he feels that it will be spiritually profitable."

Charles decided to stay and make the two villages his parish. He was consumed with a zeal for souls and he couldn't miss an opportunity to make Christ present in so pagan a land.

Meanwhile, the war had broken out between the Iroquois and the Hurons and each year the Iroquois made more and more inroads into Huron territory. Operating from their headquarters in upstate New York, centered between Rochester and Albany, they crossed the Niagara frontier in ever-increasing numbers. The French, whether traders or missionaries, were not safe from their attack.

The prime ministers of France, would not send troops to guard the settlers and missionaries the way the Spanish did. In settling California, for instance, Father Junipero Serra was held back from starting many more missions only because there weren't enough soldiers to go along.

The Spanish crown insisted that there be a definite ratio between settlers, friars and soldiery. As it was, Serra dotted the coast of California with his missions, and he received generous financial cooperation.

The Jesuits of Canada were on their own. They could not, like Serra, send demands to a governor for additional military men to support their cause.

Charles was especially devoted to the children,
and he gathered them around him for
catechism at every opportunity.

The governors of New France were fine Christian gentlemen, but they simply did not have the backing of the government in Paris.

When the Iroquois made gains in Huronia, the Jesuits could only follow their harassed flock into exile. Finally, the Jesuits moved the remnants of the Huron nation to a refuge near Quebec where there was some protection.

CHAPTER 8

MASSACRE

The Iroquois chiefs voted to invade the territory of the Petuns. They gathered their main force together to strike at the heart of the Petun strength, planning to wipe out their enemy.

The Petuns, however, were ready for them. War fever was at a high pitch, and there were almost daily war dances. Their sorcerers assured them that the gods would grant them success and that the time had come to stop the Iroquois.

A party estimated at three hundred braves was reported heading straight for St. John's village. The local chiefs gathered their men together and went out to stalk the enemy.

The Iroquois, however, were skilled veterans of war. Their main force circled around behind the village. As soon as the Petuns left, looking for them, the Iroquois descended on the defenseless village for a tremendous massacre.

Father Charles Garnier was, of course, the only Jesuit there. Women and children from several villages had been gathered there since the Petuns were confident that they could hold the place. When the Iroquois war cry sounded, Garnier was in a cabin instructing some of the people.

At the sound of the alarm, he rushed out and went straight to the church. The handful of Christians had gathered there.

"We are dead men, brothers," he said to them. "Pray to God and flee by whatever way you can."

He gave them his blessing and left hurriedly to see where he could be of help. Some found a means of escape, and they begged him to come with them.

"No," he replied. "I must remain here."

His black robes flying, he seemed to be everywhere. He gave absolution to the Christians he met. He rushed into burning cabins to rescue children. In the very midst of the flames, he poured the waters of holy Baptism for anyone who asked it.

It was while he was doing this priestly work, forgetting himself, that he was hit by two bullets. One struck him right below the breast, the other hit his thigh. He fell to the ground, and the Iroquois who had shot him fell on him and stripped him of everything. Then the Indian fled.

Charles joined his hands in prayer. The grace of martyrdom had been given to him and he offered his life for his people.

Then he looked around him. A few feet away a young brave lay dying. Charles struggled to his knees and began crawling toward the Indian. He

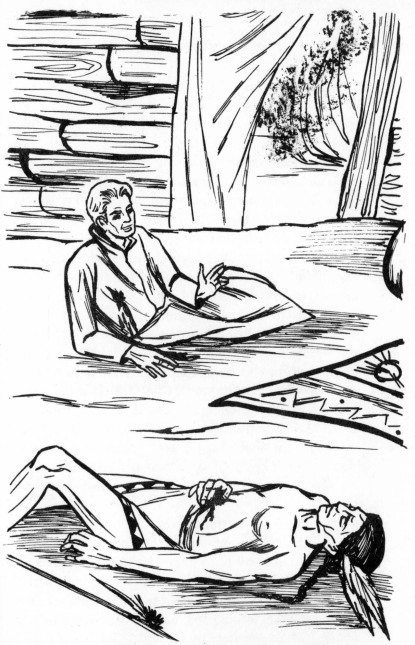

A few feet away a young brave lay dying.
Charles struggled to his knees
and began crawling toward the Indian.

went half way, and fell to the ground again. Again he tried to struggle forward. Weakened by loss of blood, his body did not have the strength of his courage and he fell, for the last time, dead.

St. Charles Garnier was martyred on the eve of the feast of the Immaculate Conception, December 7, 1649. He had often asked for the intercession of Mary to help him remain on the Cross with Christ. He had said as much in his last letter to his Carmelite brother. "May she help me become a victim to be immolated for the salvation of souls." It was fitting, indeed, that his birthday to eternity should be made in the care of the holy Mother of God.

The day after his death was a day of terror for the whole region, for no one knew where the Iroquois would strike next. The Petun braves had been surprised by the enemy, and those who had not been killed had fled in disarray. Everyone was demoralized. The Iroquois killed until they tired of it, then gathered up their booty, and retreated to enjoy themselves. They took captive many of the younger people, some to torture to death, some to become slaves.

As soon as possible, after the reign of terror, two Jesuits made their way to the ruins of St. John's.

"We found his body," they told Brebeuf, "naked and horribly mangled. We wept as we covered him."

They buried his body hurriedly, for fear the enemy might return, making plans for a decent funeral at a later date.

During 1648 and 1649, eight Jesuits gave their lives in the service of Christ and neighbor. St. John Brebeuf and St. Isaac Jogues suffered incredible torments and torture before they were allowed to die. St. Anthony Daniel, St. Gabriel Lalemant and St. Noel Chabenel fell under the blows of the Iroquois, in a manner similar to St. Charles Garnier.

Two laymen who were associated with the Jesuit activity are counted among the eight. St. Rene Goupil and St. John Lalande had volunteered to come to New France and give their lives to the service of Christ. Rene Goupil is a very interesting person in his own right, and too little known.

He had been a Jesuit seminarian but in the course of his training, it became apparent to him that he did not have a vocation. He therefore asked how he could be of service. When he saw the constant appeals for doctors in the new colonies, he studied medicine to prepare himself for the mission.

He came to Huronia to tend the sick, and to train the Jesuits to handle first aid. He was the first of the Jesuit Martyrs of North America to be put to death.

Their feast day is September 26.

CHAPTER 9

THE COMPLETED GIFT

The life of St. Charles Garnier, like that of any martyr, is an appeal to all succeeding generations for real Christian fortitude in the practice of Christ-like living. That poor human nature can rise to such heights of heroic love is encouragement to all of us in the midst of lesser trials or disappointments.

God's grace can supply strength when human nature itelf would only tremble or run away. In the Mystical Body, the sufferings of each member are joined to the sacrifice of Christ. There they are offered to God the Father in a continuing sacrifice of praise.

"That I might make up in my body what is lacking in the sufferings of Christ," is the dramatic way that St. Paul puts it. Nothing is lacking in the sacrifice of Our Lord except our union with Him.

The history of St. Charles Garnier as an individual saint points up the joyfulness of Christian living. During many years of acute suffering and deprivation, he never lost his cheerfulness, his gentleness or his sense of humor.

When St. Noel Chabanel was discouraged and was thinking of returning to France, he turned to Charles Garnier.

"I can't eat the native food and I am positively revolted by the Indian customs," said Chabanel.

"Why, back in France, our relatives spend good money to go out hunting and roughing it," replied Charles. "Here the good Lord provides it for us freely."

At each step of the way, Charles was an actual grace for his brethren. His smile encouraged them through dark and difficult times, and that same smile attracted the Indians to listen to the word of God.

"Joy," says the Abbot Marmion, "is the echo of the God-life in us." Charles became an active channel of grace, letting the God-life in him come out to be shared by all around him.

Many works of Christian charity are performed every day in schools, hospitals and social centers, but the impact of that charity is often lost when it is hidden behind a bleak and cheerless face. Charles Garnier has a message for all of these people: "Serve the Lord with joy and gladness!"

Charles found his strength in Christ, and in Him alone. Except for the companionship of Father Pierre Chastelain, Charles had no human consolations at all. Love of God and love of neighbor were his only motivation. In extending the Kingdom of God he saw the opportunity to prove his love for God and to serve Christ in his neighbor.

The Indians were certainly the least of Christ's brethren at that time. Charles repeated to himself and the other Black Robes those solemn words of Christ's, "Whatever you do to the least of these, my brethren, you do unto Me."

Not many men and women are called to serve the poor in foreign lands. That is not the message of a St. Charles Garnier. We can be distracted from the real meaning of his life if all we understand is the dramatic detail of Indian living.

Garnier encourages us to be interested in the Christian social apostolate wherever the opportunity offers itself to us. Wherever there is poverty, prejudice or injustice, Christ suffers again. "I was hungry and you fed me, sick and you visited me, naked and you clothed me. . . ."

Charles and the other great North American Martyrs saw Christ under the savage war paint of the inhabitants of Ontario and New York. They remind us that we must see Christ in every part of the world where people are in need.

And Charles Garnier reminds us that when we do give ourselves to Christ in the service of others, "The Lord loves a cheerful giver!"